A Perfect 10

10 Piano Solos in 10 Styles

Melody Bober

What could be more exhilarating than receiving the score of a perfect "10"? Olympic athletes, as well as competitors in sports, dance, and music, strive for those high marks. In fact, we all work to achieve perfection in the activities we enjoy. Wouldn't it be wonderful to find a resource that offers pianists a chance to shine at any level—solos in all styles and from all periods of music history that promote technical skills and offer the dream to succeed in performance?

Introducing *A Perfect 10*, Book 3, a collection of solos designed to promote musical excellence for the early-intermediate pianist. I chose a favorite teaching piece from the four stylistic periods—Baroque, Classical, Romantic, and Contemporary. I then wrote six original pieces in jazz, blues, ragtime, Latin, ballad, and showstopper styles. These 10 solos provide students with technical challenges as well as expressive opportunities for musical growth in mood, rhythm, melody, harmony, form, articulation, and dynamics.

You do not have to be an Olympic hopeful to achieve a perfect "10," but you might feel like one as you practice and perform these selections!

Best wishes for successful music making,

CONTENTS

Copyright © 2013 by Alfred Music
All rights reserved
ISBN-10: 0-7390-9842-X
ISBN-13: 978-7390-9842-4

Cool Cats

Jazz

Melody Bober

Sassy Samba

Latin

Melody Bober

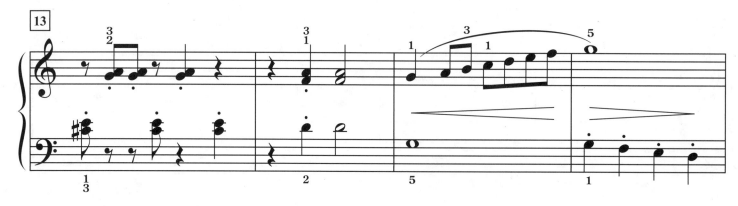

Winter Memories

Ballad

Melody Bober

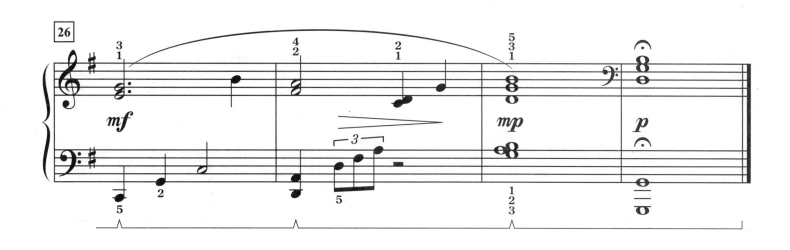

Blue Sky Rag

Ragtime

Melody Bober

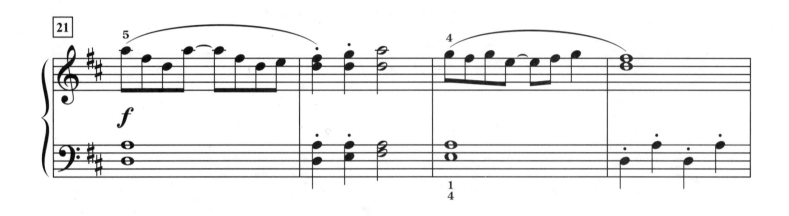

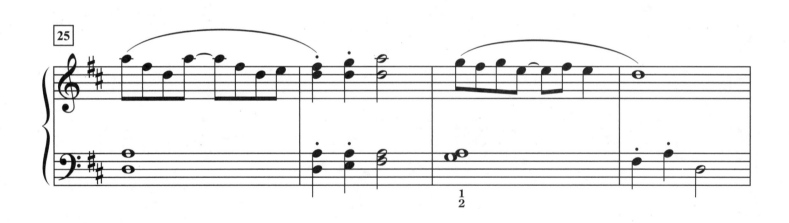

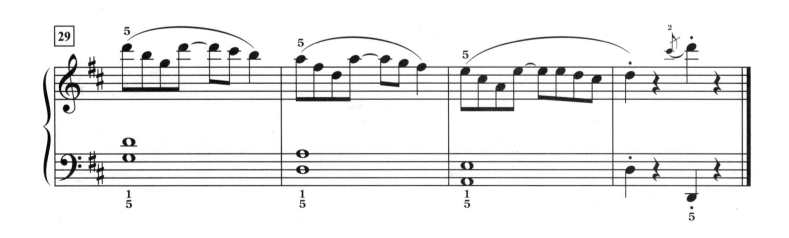

Snake Charmer Blues

Blues

Melody Bober

Spring Storm

Showstopper

Melody Bober

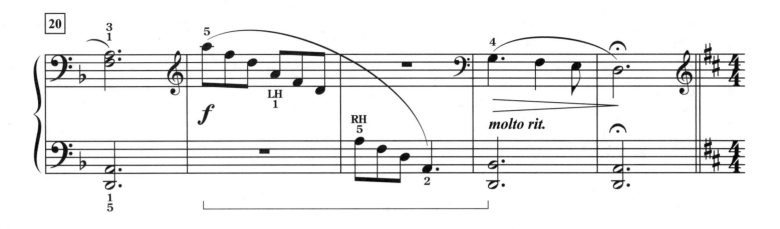

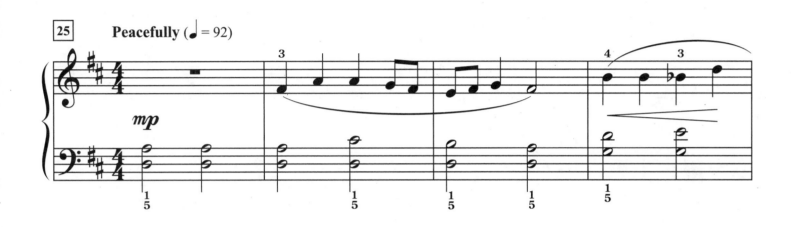

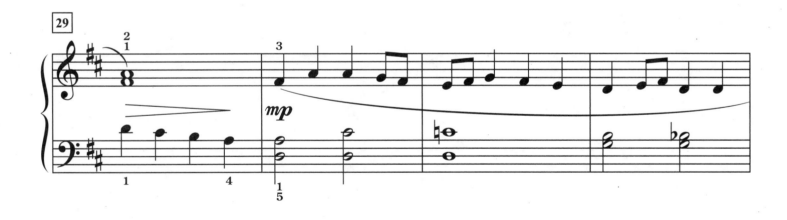

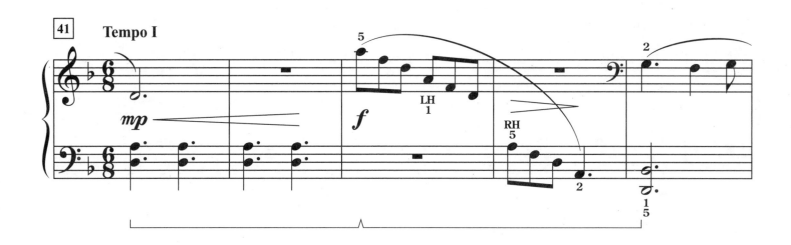

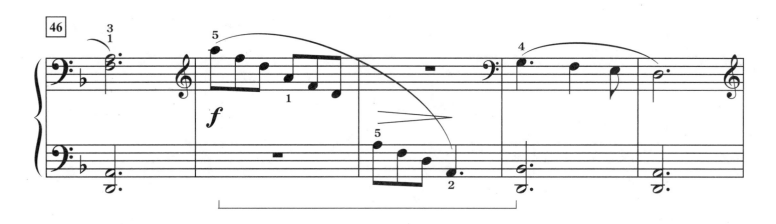

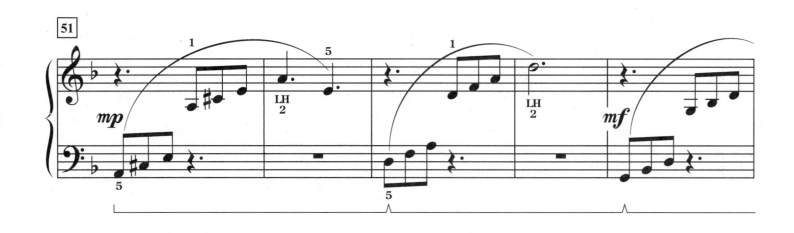

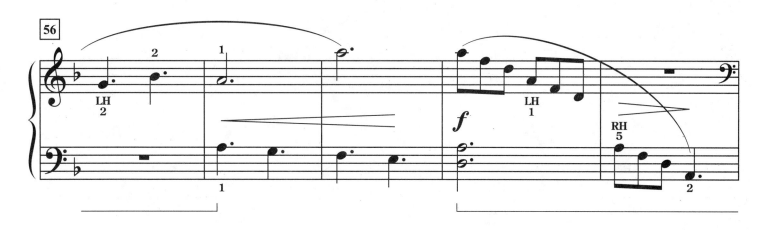

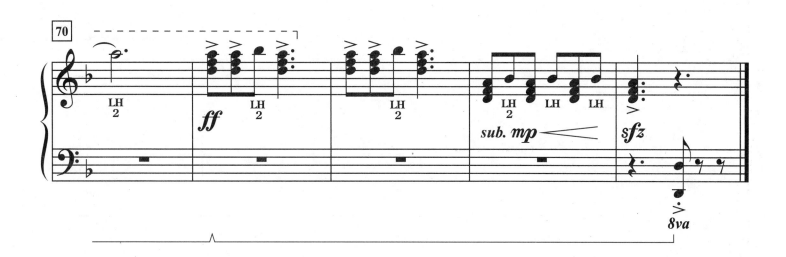

Minuet in D Minor
(Notebook for Anna Magdalena Bach)

Baroque

Johann Sebastian Bach
(1685–1750)

Allegro moderato

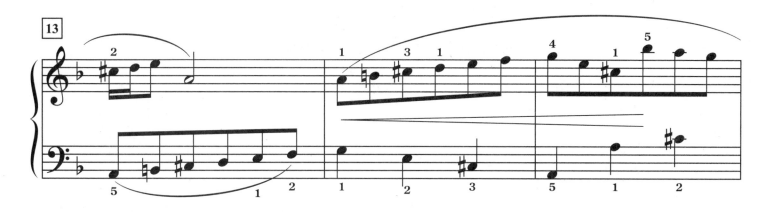

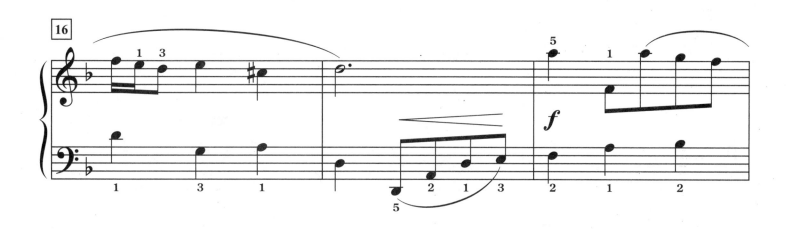

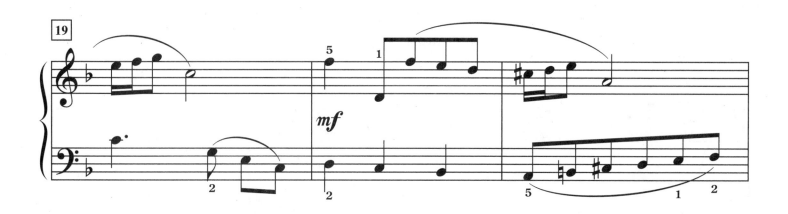

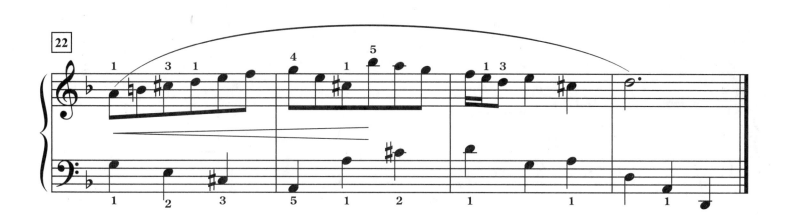

Sonatina in C Major

Classical

Theodore Latour
(1766–1837)

Arabesque

Romantic

Johann Burgmüller (1806–1874)
Op. 100, No. 2

The Village Maidens
(For Children, Volume 1)

Contemporary

Béla Bartók
(1881–1945)

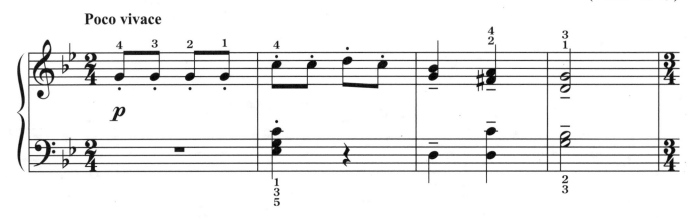

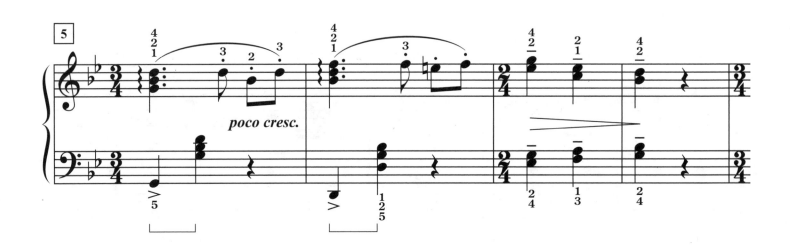

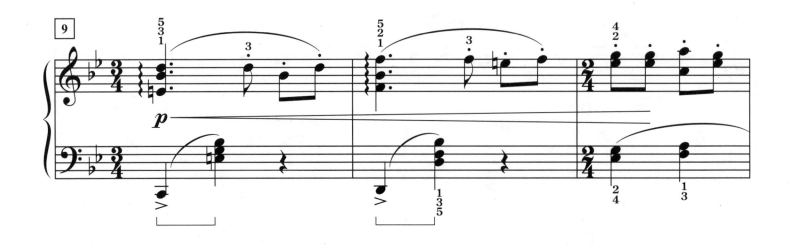

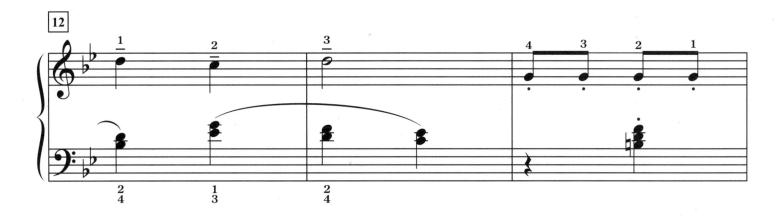

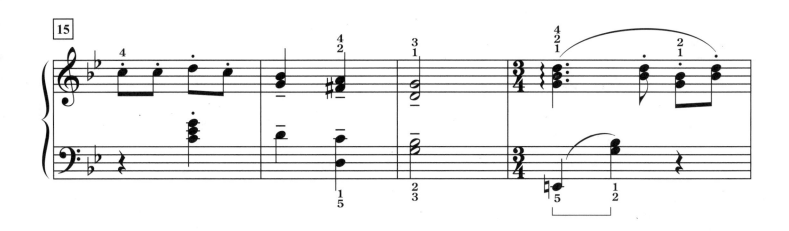

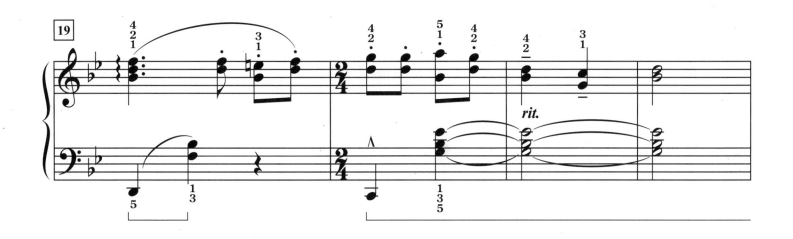